How I Do My Homework

by Jennifer Boothroyd

first step nonfiction

Lerner Publications Company · Minneapolis

The images in this book are used with the permission of: © Todd Strand/Independent Picture Service.

Front Cover: © Todd Strand/Independent Picture Service.

Main body text set in ITC Avant Garde Gothic Std Medium 21/25.
Typeface provided by Adobe Systems.

Lerner Publications Company
A division of Lerner Publishing Group, Inc.
241 First Avenue North
Minneapolis, MN 55401 USA

For reading levels and more information, look up this title at www.lernerbooks.com.

Library of Congress Cataloging-in-Publication Data

Boothroyd, Jennifer, 1972-
    How I do my homework / by Jennifer Boothroyd.
        pages   cm. — (First step nonfiction – responsibility in action)
    Includes index.
    ISBN 978–1–4677–3633–6 (lib. bdg. : alk. paper)
    ISBN 978–1–4677–3651–0 (eBook)
    1. Homework—Juvenile literature. 2. Study skills—Juvenile literature. I. Title.
LB1048.B66 2014
371.30281—dc23   2013028494

Manufactured in the United States of America
1 – BP – 12/31/13

Table of Contents

Checking for Homework

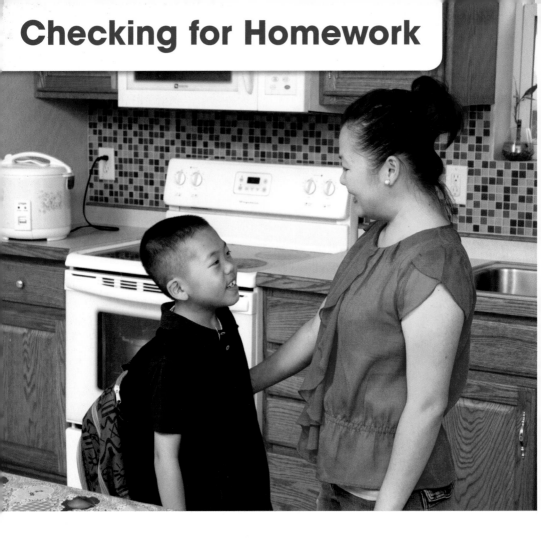

School is over. Do I have **homework**?

I look in my **backpack**.

Then I read my **planner**.

I have two **assignments**
to do.

Getting Ready to Work

First, I find a quiet place.

Next, I get everything
I need to work.

I sharpen my pencil.

Then I set out my math worksheet.

Finally, I set out my spelling list.

First, I do my math problems.

Then I **practice** writing my spelling words.

I check my work.

I cross out the assignments
I did.

Finally, I put my things back
in my backpack. I will turn
in my work tomorrow.

That's how I did my homework.

How would you do it?

Activity

Write a Story

Pretend that you are responsible for completing homework that is due tomorrow. On a separate sheet of paper, write a story about the steps that you would take to do this job. Use at least three of the words shown on the opposite page to write your story.

Story Word List

first

next

then

last

before

after

finally

Fun Facts

- In 1901, homework was banned in California. Teachers were not allowed to give homework to their students until after eighth grade!

- It's best to keep your backpack as light as possible. If your backpack is too heavy, it could cause back pain or other problems.

- Writing down your assignments in a planner is a great way to keep track of them!

Glossary

assignments – jobs given to someone to finish

backpack – a bag worn on a person's back

homework – work given by a teacher that a student finishes at home

planner – a notebook used to keep track of schoolwork

practice – to do something over and over in order to get better at it

Index